Kids' Stuff

A Workbook about Children Who are Special in Different Ways

text by Burt G. Wasserman

illustrated by A.E. Reed, III

Copyright 1999

Burt G. Wasserman

ISBN 0-932796-93-1

All rights reserved. Printed in the United States of America. The information and artwork contained herein is the exclusive property of the author. No part of this workbook may be used or reproduced in any form or by any means, or stored in a database or retrieval system, without prior written permission of the author except in the case of brief quotations embodied in critical articles and reviews. Making copies of any part of this workbook for any purpose other than your own personal use is a violation of United States copyright laws.

This workbook is sold or otherwise provided *as is*, without warranty of any kind, either express or implied, respecting the contents of this workbook, including but not limited to implied warranties for the workbook's quality, performance, merchantability, or fitness for any particular purpose. Neither the workbook's authors, publishers, nor distributors shall be liable to the purchaser or any other person or entity with respect to any liability, loss, or damage caused or alleged to be caused directly or indirectly by this workbook.

Library of Congress Catalog Card No. 99-60609

Printing (Last Digit

9 8 7 6 5 4 3 2 1

Publisher—

Educational Media Corporation®
PO Box 21311
Minneapolis, MN 55421-0311

(612) 781-0088

For Educational Media Corporation—

Production editor—

Don L. Sorenson

Graphic Design—

Earl R. Sorenson

A Workbook about Children Who are Special in Different Ways

Introduction for Adults

We all deal with many issues as we grow up. At times, children who are hurting emotionally have to deal with life issues before they have attained the developmental level where they normally would be equipped to do so.

One purpose of this workbook is to help children deal with issues that they might be forced to confront because of certain circumstances in their lives.

A second purpose is to familiarize *all* children regarding these "special" issues. These are tough issues dealing with strong emotions that are usually dealt with by parents, teachers, and counselors. Therefore, this workbook is also a prevention tool. Instead of rescuing children after they fall in the river, the material presented may teach them to swim or at least equip them with a life preserver until help arrives.

Written for parents, teachers, and counselors, this workbook is to be used *with* children from the ages of 6 to 12. For some children it may prepare them to be more tolerant and empathic to other children who are different from them. For other children it may provide coping strategies to deal with life stresses they may be going through.

The message of this book for all children is that they are not alone and that just because they are small doesn't mean they have to be the victims of any form of abuse. It is also designed to promote empathy and understanding with the goal of reducing cruelty among children.

Because so many different issues are addressed, this workbook also can be used by counselors as a screening tool to get individual children talking about subjects that previously have not been discussed.

Table of Contents

1. Being a Kid 7
2. Growing Up Too Quickly 12
3. That Hopeless Feeling 16
4. When Parents Need Help 21
5. When Families Change 25
6. There are Many Types of Families 28
7. Wondering About Your Birth Parents 29
8. For Children Who Don't Think They are Smart 32
9. When Children Learn Differently 36
10. Being Different from Other Children 38
11. Children Who are Hyperactive 40
12. When Children Take Medicine 44
13. Dealing with a Loss 49
14. When Bad Things Happen to Good People 56
15. Dealing with Anger 58
16. Dealing with Nightmares 64
17. Dealing with Fears 70
18. From Now On 77

Introduction for Children

This is a workbook about children who are having hard times. If you are one of these children, it may help to learn that you are not alone. You may also learn that any problems you are dealing with now may make you stronger and wiser once you learn how to handle them.

One important way of dealing with a problem is to talk to someone about it. If you have been keeping your problem a secret, it would be a good idea to talk to your teacher or counselor.

This workbook is also for children who don't have any big problems. Hopefully the workbook will help you to understand some of your classmates. If you understand some of the "special situations" they are going through, perhaps you will be more understanding and tolerant of their circumstances and less likely to engage in teasing and cruelty.

Talking about another's problems is not a good thing for you to do. It's called gossip or having a BIG MOUTH. Remember to leave any discussion of other's problems in the classroom or the counseling office and not blab it all over the school. Do you think you can handle that responsibility? Great!

Now, let's take a look at what it means to be a kid, and what makes some kids "special in different ways."

About the Author

Burt Wasserman *is a licensed professional counselor in the State of Virginia with 25 years of experience working with children. He has been a national presenter on the top of brief therapy with children and also is the author of **Stories for Children with Problems and Wishes: A Therapeutic Workbook for Turning Problems into Gifts** and **Feeling Good Again: A Workbook for Children Who have been Sexually Abused**.*

His belief is that children are capable of a deeper understanding of things than many adults might think they can handle. This level of understanding can help children deal with their problems, and as a result, become wiser and stronger.

Mr. Wasserman is the proud father of two children, Greg and Pam, and the grandfather of Anna Camille.

A Workbook about Children Who are Special in Different Ways

Being a Kid
Everybody should have a chance to be one.

Kids' Stuff

*Being a kid is an important job. The main things you have to learn are to treat other people in a nice way, to do your best in school, and to have **fun**!*

Your job as a kid isn't to worry about things or to be "the man of the house."

*Just as you wouldn't tell a two-year-old to go outside and shovel the snow, **you shouldn't be doing and worrying about grown up things.***

Sometimes children are forced to grow up too fast.

They have to cook for their family, take care of their brothers and sisters, and worry about their parents.

For some children their lives become hard instead of fun.

Their lives may be hard because of where they live, the color of their skin, the problems of their parents, or their own problems.

Remember, even though you may be experiencing some hard times, you are still a kid and one of your jobs is to have fun.

A Workbook about Children Who are Special in Different Ways

Draw a picture of yourself doing your favorite thing and having fun. If you don't have a chance to have much fun, draw a picture of something you would like to be doing so you could have fun.

Kids' Stuff

You are not alone. Lots of other kids have problems, too.

Some of their problems may be bigger than yours—some may be smaller. But, all children have some problems to handle.

One thing that might surprise you about problems is that they are not all bad.

When you have a problem, one thing is for sure—learning how to handle your problems will make you stronger, wiser, and better able cope with the next difficult time that comes your way.

One of the main ideas of this workbook is to help you to learn to see your problem differently so you can deal with it more effectively and turn your problem into a gift.

When your problem has been turned into a gift, you can begin to see what you have learned and how you have become stronger and wiser.

Draw a picture of your confused self before you figured out how to deal with your problem.

A Workbook about Children Who are Special in Different Ways

Now, draw a picture of what you want to look like after you have turned that problem into a gift.

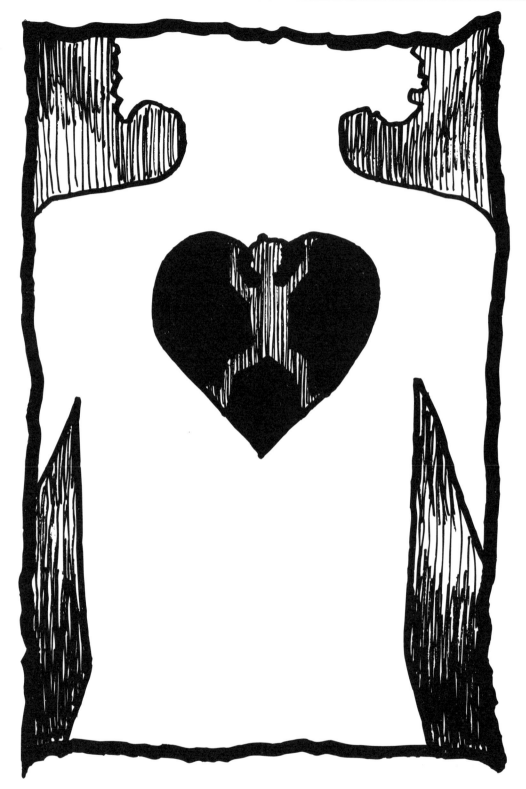

Growing Up Too Quickly
When things in your life prevent you from being a kid.

Some children have to grow up too quickly for many reasons. Some have to be baby-sitters or a cook, others have to be the "man of the house." Some even believe they have to keep a parent from drinking or using drugs.

Do you share any of these problems?

If you have to deal with these "adult" tasks, you don't have any time for doing kids' stuff!

Draw a picture of yourself doing the thing that prevents you from doing kids' stuff.

Kids' Stuff

Sometimes it's hard to do kids' stuff.

What kids' stuff would you like to do if you had the time?

Is there anyone you would like to do it with?

Draw a picture of yourself doing kids' stuff.

The purpose of this book is to help you find time to do more of the kid's stuff you would like to do.

Do you know anybody you can talk to who can help you to do more of the things you would like to do as a kid?

Has anybody else told you that you need to be a kid?

What questions do you think kids have who have to grow up too quickly?

That Hopeless Feeling
When things feel like they will never change.

Many children, at one time or another, have had a hopeless feeling that things are never going to change.

When children get that feeling it's as if they were in a tunnel with no light and no clue when they might reach the end.

Some children get that feeling because they feel different from everybody else. Other children feel hopeless because one of their parents drink too much or uses drugs.

Other children feel hopeless because their classmates are mean to them.

Sometimes children don't even know why they feel hopeless or crummy all the time.

Have you ever felt hopeless or crummy?

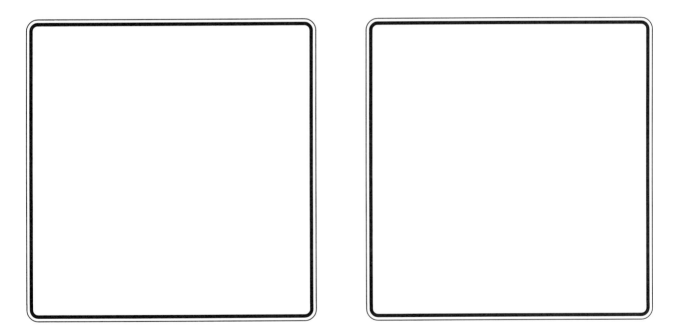

If you feel that way now, draw a picture of what makes you feel hopeless. Then, draw what you would like to have happen to make that feeling go away.

Did you know that children can get that hopeless feeling when other kids are mean to them?

Have you ever been mean to another child?

Did you realize how much it hurt that person?

Now that you know how others might feel, maybe you might be less likely to be mean to someone else.

The reason your drawings are important is so you can remember them if the hopeless feeling comes again.

You can remember how things can and did change.

Adults call that hopeless feeling **depression.** *Depression is when you just give up.*

Some children even say, "I wish I were dead!"

Did you ever feel that way?

When children say they want to die, they really just want the pain to stop. What they need to remember is to HANG ON, because things will get better.

Sometimes you have to wait a while until you can see things differently.

*Draw two pictures. The first picture can be of the problem **you used to have in the past** (or the one you would like to put in the past).*

Your second picture can be of when the problem changed (or how you would like it to change) so you no longer felt that you wanted to die.

Some children believe that when they die, they will join their loved ones in heaven. Others believe the loved ones who have died are very lonely and need company. No one really knows for sure what happens after we die. However, the thing you need to remember is that it is normal to feel like you may want to, but the neat part is sticking around to see how things turn out on **Earth.**

Some people believe that the most important Heaven is the **Heaven on Earth.** *They believe that if you are kind and loving, most other people will treat you in a kind and loving way. That is what they believe is Heaven on Earth.*

What do you think?

A Workbook about Children Who are Special in Different Ways

When Parents Need Help
And you don't feel safe.

Kids' Stuff

Sometimes children are sad because they worry about one of their parents.

Some children are afraid to go to sleep because their father drinks too much alcohol and they are afraid what might happen.

Other children worry about their mother being hit by their father, while others are afraid of getting hit themselves.

Are their times you worry about one of your parents?

Draw a picture that shows the thing you worry most about in one box, and what that picture will look like when there is no longer a problem.

What you may have to learn is that it is not your job to worry about your parents or to make sure they are safe.

The tough thing about this is, when your parents have problems, as much as you may want to fix their problems, you are not able to do it for them.

Your parents can't really make you eat your peas or study in school, and you won't be able to change them by yourself.

However, you can change yourself. You can learn to feel safe rather than to be worried or scared.

If you don't feel safe, you need to talk to a parent first. If that doesn't help, you need to talk to someone else—a counselor or another adult that you trust.

Sometimes it is something a parent does that causes you not to feel comfortable or safe.

Parents are not supposed to be touching you in ways that make you feel uncomfortable. They shouldn't be punching or slapping you or throwing you around.

And they shouldn't be calling you names like "dumb" or "stupid." Words like those from parents really hurt!

Some parents need to see a counselor and to find out how to treat their children.

Kids' Stuff

It may be scary to talk to someone else about your parent. It may feel that you are going behind your parent's back. But, you need to protect yourself, and most parents would like to get along better with their children—if they knew how.

Some parents even may have to go to court because of the way they are treating their children.

Most children look to their parents to protect them, but if that is not working, you should know that there are many other adults in your life that care about you and want to keep you safe.

Make a list of all the adults that you can think of that care about you and want to keep you safe.

_____   _____

_____   _____

_____   _____

_____   _____

_____   _____

_____   _____

A Workbook about Children Who are Special in Different Ways

When Families Change
A family is a group of people who love you.

Educational Media Corporation®, Box 21311, Minneapolis, MN 55421-0311

*All families are different, especially **blended** families. A blended family is one where a single parent marries another single parent and both parents bring their children together to make one big blended family. When this happens, getting along with other family members can be a major problem.*

Some children don't like their new step parent and others find it difficult to get along with their step sisters or brothers.

People who study families report that it often takes a few years for step brothers and sisters to feel like they are part of a family again.

To these kids it might seem like a long time, but things do change.

When you are having a difficult time with another member of the family, it helps to try to think about what the other person might be feeling.

If you imagine how the other person might feel, it may be easier for you to change the way you treat that person.

So, the next time you are having a fight with a member of your family—or anybody else for that matter—ask yourself this question.

Would I want someone else to treat me the way I'm treating this person?

If you answered that question with a "no," as you think about it, you would probably change your behavior. You also have demonstrated that you have a special quality called **empathy**. *Empathy is when you consider other people's feelings when you make a decision.*

Each time you ask yourself that question you will be increasing the amount of empathy that you have for others. You will also be a much nicer person and you will attract other nice people.

There are Many Types of Families

All families are different. The most important thing is that there is love in your family.

Single Parent Families—

Having only one parent may be difficult for some children, but they are not alone. There are many children who come from single parent homes.

*Nevertheless, it is still no fun when Fathers' Day comes around and your father is **not** around.*

Same Sex Parents—

Some children have two parents that are the same sex. Sometimes these parents love each other in the same way a mother and father love each other. Sometimes their children get teased when both parents are of the same sex. They hear others call their parents "gay," or names that are meant to be put downs.

If you have two parents of the same sex, the important thing to remember is that it is how much each loves you that matters and not what others say because they are different.

People often call other people nasty names because they don't like anything that is different.

If you don't understand the relationship of your same sex parents, you may want to ask them some questions which they should be happy to answer.

A Workbook about Children Who are Special in Different Ways

Wondering About Your Birth Parents
And the feeling that goes with not knowing.

Some children live with foster parents or adoptive parents. These are parents who have chosen their children rather than becoming birth parents.

*For these children, the parents they live with **are** their real parents because they are the ones who sat up with them when they were sick, hugged them when they needed hugs, and fed and clothed them.*

If you are one of these children, you may also wonder about your birth parents.

These thoughts are normal and often painful if you don't know where your birth parents are.

So, at times, being an adopted or a foster child may not seem like so much fun.

These are the times that you may want to look at the brighter side of things. It's like looking at the glass of soda below. Is it half empty or half full?

*Both answers are correct. When you say something is half full, it **seems like** it is more.*

Sometimes in order to feel happier, we have to look at the brighter (half full) side of things.

Having one or two loving parents is a whole lot better than not having any parents. And having parents that have time for you is better than having parents that don't have any time.

Can you think of the brighter side in your family?

Draw a picture of something that represents the brighter side of your family.

For Children Who Don't Think They are Smart
There are many ways to be smart.

Which children do you think are "smart?"

Are they children who can read, write, and do arithmetic well?

Do they know how to be nice and keep their friends?

Are you smart if you can look at a tree and draw it so well it looks like a photograph?

Are they the ones who know which pitches to swing at and have high batting averages because of their skills?

What do you think?

Some children don't get good grades in school, but they can do other things well. Does that mean they are not smart?

Children learn differently, and because of that, some do well at school and some do well on the playground.

Some children do well when they have a paint brush and others do well while they have a musical instrument. There are many ways to be smart. It is unfair to say someone is not smart just because he or she doesn't do well in school.

We all learn some things easier than we learn others. Children who are good at reading and math may not be very good at building model airplanes or playing basketball.

Other children don't do well in school and don't have any special talents, except that they have a big smile on their face and they spread love and joy everywhere. They may not be smart, but they are special in other ways.

*The point is that everybody should be treated with **mutual respect** and not be looked down upon because they don't do well in school.*

So far we have talked about kids who do okay in school. But, there are some children who can't learn as well as others because their brains are different. Some of these children even look different. These children are "mentally challenged" because they have to work so hard to learn certain things.

Unfortunately, they get teased at times because they are different. At other times the word "retard" is used as a put down.

These children have feelings just like you, but put downs may hurt them even more because they don't know how to fight back with words. If they did, they probably wouldn't say anything mean because they are so kind. They wouldn't want to hurt anyone else's feelings.

What do you think about yourself? Do you think you are smart? Are you one of those kids who has a hard time at school? If you are, I hope you have learned that there are many ways to be special; doing well in school is just one of those ways.

Are there other ways that you think you are smart? In what ways are you special?

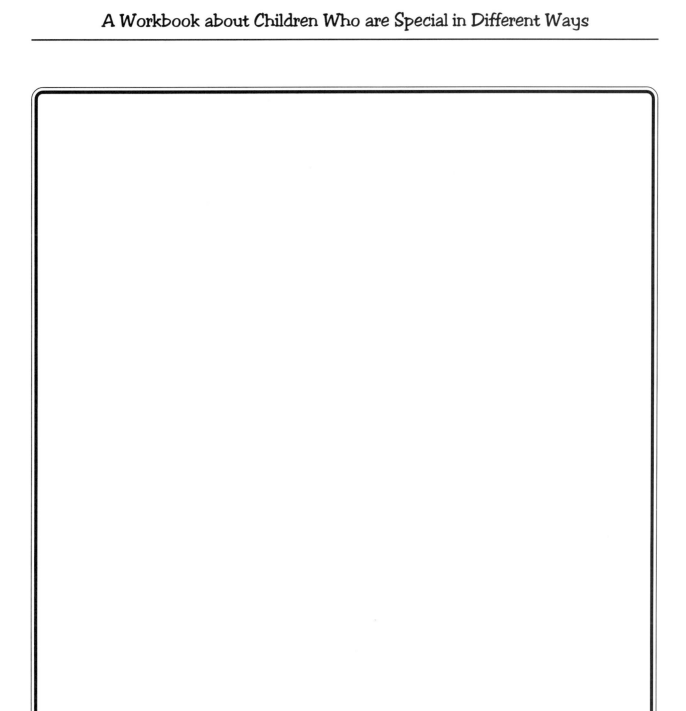

Draw a picture of yourself surrounded by the words that make you special.

When Children Learn Differently
You can be very smart and still have a learning disability.

We all learn differently.

*Some of us learn better when we can hear the directions, others when we can read them, and still others when we are shown how to do something. Children who have a hard time learning the way the teacher introduces a subject are said to have a **learning disability.***

*Some people think that is the wrong name and that the correct name should be a **teacher disability,** because the teacher hasn't been able to teach the child. What do you think?*

Some children who have a learning disability get down on themselves and think of themselves as being stupid. Guess what? Nothing could be farther from the truth, because most children who have learning disabilities are usually pretty smart.

Do you know of any famous people who have a learning disability? Ask your teacher or counselor about it.

As you get older, your learning disability may not be as much of a problem because you may learn how to deal with it. The most important thing to remember if you have a learning disability is that you are not alone. There are many children who have a learning disability, so there is no need to feel any shame.

There are many different kinds of learning disabilities. Some kids have problems with reading and are a whiz at math. Others are great with reading and writing stories, but they hate to work with numbers.

Kids' Stuff

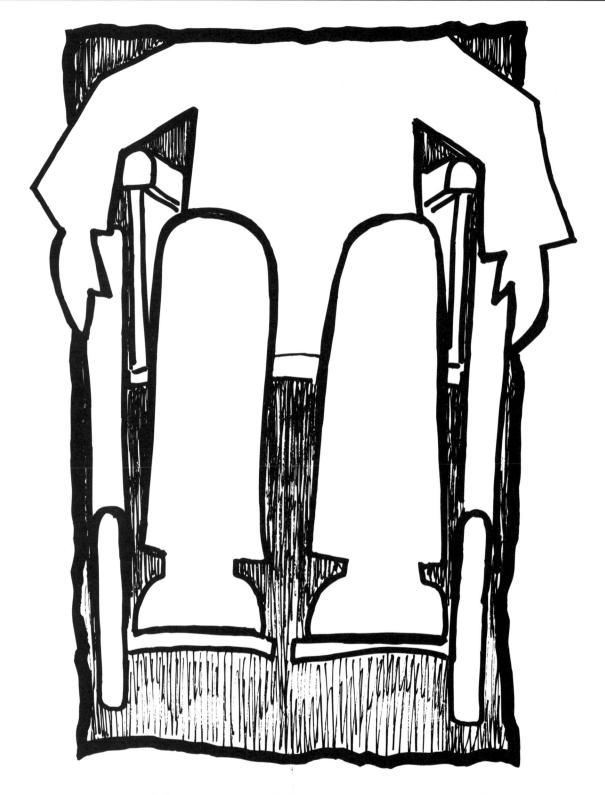

Being Different from Other Children
Children with handicaps are the real heroes.

Some children have parents who have a different skin color than they have. Although there is nothing wrong with that, other children may say mean things to these children.

If this is happening to you, it must really hurt.

Children are usually cruel when they are hurting inside themselves or are angry about something. They think being angry at someone else will get their anger out and make them feel better, but it doesn't work!

Remember, taking your anger out on someone else by being mean and cruel only makes you a meaner person; it will never really make you feel better.

The children who need wheelchairs to get around or those that have difficulty walking, as a result of an accident or illness, are the real heroes of your school.

Each and every day they go to school, they have challenges that the rest of us don't have.

Despite all they go through, sometimes they get teased.

If others knew what it was like to have a physical disability, they would never tease them.

Remember, empathy is different from sympathy. Children with disabilities don't want to be pitied, they just want to be understood.

Children with disabilities just want to be treated the same as everybody else. You can probably even tease them in a playful manner—just don't tease them about their disability.

Children Who are Hyperactive
It's not easy being me.

Children who are "hyper" can be real problems in school. Sometimes it's so hard for them to keep still that they become class clowns to cover up their difficulties.

Those children who are allowed to take medicine often find that the medicine makes it easier for them to calm down. If you are a child who is hyperactive, you know that it isn't easy to stay calm in school.

Not all hyperactive children are allowed to take medicine, so others need to have understanding and empathy for them and realize that they are probably doing the best they can.

Even though it's difficult to calm down, the exercise on the next page can be helpful.

Start by imagining that there is a calm feeling helper standing over one shoulder, and the "hyper" feeling distracter over the other.

Close your eyes to make the following choice.

> *Choose a cool, calm color for your helper and a wild, crazy color for your distracter. Color both figures.*
>
> *The **first** thing to do to bring the calm feeling in by imaging that the calm color is coming into your body as you take long, slow, deep breaths.*
>
> *The **second** thing is to pretend that you can actually feel the calm feeling coming into your body.*
>
> *The **third** thing is to stay calm, quiet, and focused.*

Part of the reason it is so difficult to concentrate in school is that many children fill their heads with negative thoughts or "put downs" about their ability to learn. They think that they are either too slow, too stupid, or too hyper to learn. They are so busy hearing this stuff in their heads that they can't hear the teacher.

What you need to remember is to replace your "put downs" with "put ups."

Close your eyes and pick two colors—one for each of the figures below. They may be the same as your calm and hyper colors or they can be different. Next, list some of the "put downs" and some of the "put ups" you used in the past.

Put Downs   Put Ups

_____   _____

_____   _____
_____   _____

When Children Take Medicine

*Most of the kids you know who take medicine may be taking **Ritalin**. It is a medicine to help them to concentrate.*

*Some children don't like to take **Ritalin** because they say it "slows them down," and others say "it makes them feel different."*

*Most children who take **Ritalin** like themselves better when they are taking that medication. They feel they have more control of what they do or say.*

*If you are taking **Ritalin**, you may want to ask yourself whether you like yourself better when you are taking **Ritalin** or not taking it. You may want to discuss the answer with your counselor, teacher, guardian, or parent.*

*Children who use **Ritalin** have had problems with concentration and, in some cases, moving around too much. Doctors call what they have ADHD. An adult can tell you what the letters mean.*

Children who have a mild case of ADHD can use strategies (like the breathing activity in the last chapter) to help them calm down and concentrate without medication.

When you have ADHD it is as if you have a bunch of TV sets going on at the same time in your mind. Medicine helps you to focus on just one TV set—the most important thing that's going on in your life at that time. When you are in school, that is usually the teacher or the work you are assigned to be doing.

Some children who have mild cases of ADHD can learn to turn off the noise of all of the TV sets they have in their head by taking slow deep breaths and filling their bodies with the color and the calm, quiet, focused feeling that goes with that color.

Other children use a machine hooked up to a computer. When they look at the computer screen, they try to get all of their attention focused on what is happening on the screen. By doing this they change the way their brain works. This is hard work and it takes a long time to learn, but after a year of working with a counselor on the computer, many of these children no longer need medication to concentrate.

Sometimes children take medicine for other problems, like feeling really sad, hearing voices in their heads, or making movements and sounds that they can't control.

Whenever children need medicine, it is because the chemicals in their brains are not working properly. The medicine they take is supposed to take the place of the chemicals that the brain is not making enough of. Sometimes the medicine helps the brain make the chemicals it needs so the children can eventually stop taking the medicine. Other times the brain will always need some medicine to keep it working okay.

Some children take medicine because they hear voices in their heads. Sometimes these voices come when they are really sad. Medicine usually helps the voices go away. When these children stop feeling sad, the voices also stop and they can eventually stop taking their medicine. Other children can make these voices go away without medication. There are still other times when the brain can never make enough of the right chemicals. When that happens, they need to take the medication so the voices don't come back.

There are two important things to remember about taking medication. You are not alone because many children need to take medication for one reason or another. If it helps you to do better in school or with your friends, be happy that it works and thank your parents for getting you the help that you need.

A Workbook about Children Who are Special in Different Ways

Dealing with a Loss
The best thing about loved ones lives on in others.

When Things Stop Living

Flowers die and become part of the soil to enable new flowers to grow.

Draw your favorite flower in the box below.

There is a part of a flower that never dies, it just changes. We call it "energy."

Energy is in a flower when it is growing and it goes into the soil when the flower dies. The energy in the soil helps make new flowers grow.

When People Die

Most people live until they get old. Most old people have wonderful memories about their children and grandchildren. Some people like to think they can take these memories with them when they die, so they are not lonely. What do you think?

Draw a picture of one of the memories you would want one of your grandparents, aunts, or uncles to take with.

Kids' Stuff

Just as the energy from flowers lives on in other flowers, there also is energy from people that lives on in other people. We call that energy their "soul."

The people they loved will always have some of their energy or some of their soul. That is the last gift a loved one can leave with you. Your memories of that loved one is also that person's soul.

What are some memories that a loved one has left, or will leave, for you?

It's as if they never really die because the memories of them and what they taught lives on in the people they knew.

The sad thing is we can't see them or play with them again, but we can always talk to them in our heart.

Draw a picture of a love whose memory you have kept in your heart and mind.

When someone in a family dies, the children are often afraid that someone else also will die.

Sometimes they are afraid one of their parents will die.

*Please don't worry. Most parents live to get old and be grandparents so they can play with **your children.***

Draw a picture of yourself in the future as an adult, with your children and one or both of your parents. If you are living with a grandparent, you may also want to draw that person in the picture. Your grandparent will be your children's great grandparent.

*If you worry about one of your parents dying, it may be helpful to draw another picture of you and that parent in the future. Perhaps it could be when you graduate from **college** or you could draw your parent visiting you at work.*

Kids' Stuff

Sometimes when a parent dies before the children have a chance to grow up to be parents, those children also want to die so they can be with that parent. One child even thought about running in front of a car. What he didn't understand was that dying wouldn't really help.

*Some parents believe that if they died before their children were grown up, the most pleasure they could possibly have would not be to have their children visit them in Heaven, but to watch their children grow up on **Earth!***

Some people say that when you are in Heaven, you can see the future. If that is so, it may be why parents don't have to worry in Heaven because they know you are going to grow up and that everything will be okay.

Draw a picture of yourself in the future on Earth when everything will be okay.

Some people talk about not waiting to go to Heaven to change their lives. They stop worrying about things they cannot control while they are still living on Earth. They call it "Heaven on Earth."

Is there anything you worry about that you can't control?

It doesn't happen very often, but sometimes even children die. When that does happen, the hardest thing to understand is why such an awful thing happened.

There is never a good reason why children have to die.

What is important to know is that they didn't die because they were bad or because they were being punished for doing something wrong.

What also is important to understand is that when a child wishes someone was dead, it is done in anger and that person usually don't really mean it.

*As angry as a child might have been, a child could **never** cause another person to die because of a wish.*

When people die, their life stories come to an end. The people whom they loved can honor them by remembering the things that they taught them.

When Bad Things Happen to Good People

Did anything really bad ever happen to you?

If it did, did you think it was your fault?

Sometimes when bad things happen, children think there has to be a reason. If they don't know the reason, often they blame themselves.

Sometimes there is a reason and sometimes there is not.

Can you think of a time when a bad thing happened to a good person for no good reason?

Sometimes when bad things happen, people even blame God.

What do you think? Do you think God would cause a bad thing to happen?

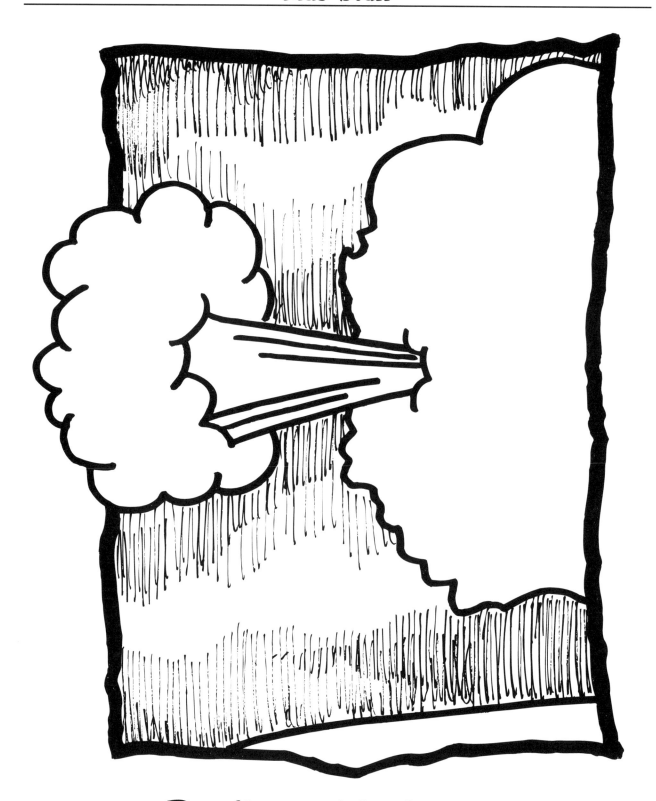

Dealing with Anger
And learning to be in control.

If you think of your anger as a machine that you can turn on and off, you will have taken the first step to controlling your anger.

Draw a picture of your anger machine.

Because your anger came so quickly in the past, you may have believed you couldn't control your anger. You may have even thought that you were a bad person.

There are many children just like you who also felt that way, but they found out they could change.

One way to change is to look at things differently. On the next page are three ways to look at anger differently.

1. *Anger is something you can control. No one else can make you angry.*

2. *Anger can be viewed as a signal to change, rather than something that has a life of its own that keeps growing and getting worse.*

3. *Your body reacts in a certain way before you get to the point where your anger is out of control. If you listen to your body, it will send cues that you are about to get really angry, unless you do something to head off the anger.*

*The **first** step to controlling your anger is **knowing your body cues.** Some children notice their fists tighten, others feel their face getting red, while others start to feel tense all over. The neat thing about your body cues is that they appear **before** your anger is out of control.*

*The **second** step to controlling your anger is **knowing your triggers.***

*Triggers are the people, places, and things that **you have reacted to in the past** in order to get your anger started.*

When children say, "He made me angry," they are mistaken, because no one can do that but yourself.

*Responding to your **body cues** and remembering your **triggers** from the past, will serve to remind you about the **third** step which is to **change your breathing.***

When you change your breathing to long, slow, deep breaths, you can bring your calm feeling into your body.

*Once the calm feeling is in your body, it will be easier to start the **fourth** step to controlling your anger which is **change your thinking.***

Remember, the reason you want to change your thinking is because that's what made you angry in the first place.

You can change your thinking in three ways.

1. **Think calm thoughts.**
2. **See calm pictures.**
3. **Remember calm words from other people.**

*The trick is to begin to change your thinking as soon as your **body cues** tell you an angry feeling is coming.*

*If you know you are about to step into a situation that might make you angry or has been a **trigger** in the past, that becomes your signal to start to **change your thinking** by running a different movie through your mind, by remembering what other people have said in the past to help you stay calm, and by saying calming things to yourself.*

The **fifth** step to controlling your anger is to **step back** out of your picture and watch what you are doing. Once you are able to do that, you will probably do a pretty good job of controlling your anger.

One way to think of this step is to imagine that you are watching a movie picture of yourself dealing with a situation so that you don't lose your temper.

Or it could be as if a part of you was looking down from above and coaching yourself to continue to use your anger management skills to stay calm.

Anger Management

The five steps to controlling anger are:
1. *Know your **body cues.***
2. *Know your **triggers.***
3. *Change your **breathing.***
4. *Change your **thinking.***
5. *Step back and **evaluate.***

Kids' Stuff

Dealing with Nightmares
Why we have them.

Burt C. Wasserman

Nightmares are bad dreams about the problems you have during the day. Often when you solve your problems during the day, your nightmares go away.

You may also have nightmares because of:

    Things that have happened to you in the past;

    Things you worry about; and

    Things you have seen in the movies or on TV.

What type of nightmares have you had?

Are you still having nightmares?

Do you think your nightmares will go away now that you have solved your problem?

A nightmare is like a bad movie that you see in your dreams.

If you watch scary movies during the day, you are more likely to have nightmares.

Kids' Stuff

*Even though nightmares are upsetting, in a way they are like other problems because **they are signals** that you need to talk to somebody or stop watching horror movies.*

Sometimes after you talk to somebody the nightmares go away.

Did that ever happen to you?

Sometimes, even after you talk to someone, the nightmares don't go away.

Draw a picture of the way you remember your nightmare.

Sometimes when you change the picture of your nightmare, the nightmare goes away.

How would you like to change your picture?

*If their is a big monster in your picture, you can make him very small and make yourself **BIG**!*

*You can draw bars over the monster so **he can't get off the paper!***

*If there are other mean people in your nightmare, you can draw them again, but this time make them **clowns!***

Sometimes children bring their favorite cartoon characters or stuffed animals into their dream to protect them and be their helpers.

Is there a helper that you would like to bring into your dream to protect you?

What could your helper be doing in the dream?

Sometimes when you add peaceful colors to your dream, the dream becomes more peaceful.

What colors would you like to add to your dream?

*Change the picture of the bad dream you had in the **past** so it becomes a funny, peaceful dream.*

Kids' Stuff

*Sometimes the monster in your dream is really a **person** dressed in a monster's clothing.*

Were there any people hiding in your dream?

Who do you think would be the best person to talk to about your dreams?

Draw a picture of yourself telling someone about your dream,

or

draw a picture of the person in your dream wearing a clown's clothes so that person is not scary anymore.

You may have had a nightmare because of something that you worried about during the day.

*Is there **anything** that you are afraid will happen?*

*Is there **anybody** that you are afraid of?*

Do you need to draw anything else into the picture of the nightmare that will allow you to feel even more safe, so the nightmare becomes just a dream that you may not even remember it the next day?

Dealing with Fears
The real ones and the ones we make up in our minds.

There are two kinds of fear: (1) the fear that is about something real, and (2) the fear that we make up in our minds.

*Real fears are good to have because they keep you safe. Most children are smart enough to be afraid of some things, like playing in the street or walking on a roof. They are also smart enough to say **no** to someone who wants them to do something dangerous.*

*Have you ever said **no** to something that was dangerous?*

Sometimes children are not really sure they should be afraid. Some children do things because they didn't look dangerous at first. Did you ever do something that didn't look dangerous?

Some children play with matches because it doesn't look dangerous. Have you ever played with matches?

When you are not sure if something is dangerous, listen to the your inner voice for an answer. And, always remember to talk to someone about it.

Sometimes children have fears of other people.

They are afraid those people will hit them or that those people will touch them in the wrong places.

Is there some person in your life that you are afraid of?

Who would be the best person to talk to about this problem?

Your counselor or your parent?

Sometimes children are **afraid to talk to someone** *because of what they think* **might** *happen.*

The same people that they are afraid of made them afraid to **tell someone.**

If you are afraid you will be hurt or something will happen to someone else if you tell someone, you are being **tricked.** *You must tell someone. There are people who will protect you!*

Sometimes children don't talk about their fears because they think no one will care, no one will believe them, or no one will listen.

If you have a problem, you need to keep talking to different people until someone does listen.

*Remember, if you have a real fear, you **must** tell someone.*

Draw a picture of any real fears you may have.

*If a real fear is one where something will **really** happen, a made up fear is one where something will only happen in your mind.*

Some children are afraid of the dark. Others are afraid of insects. And, others are even afraid of germs.

These children think something awful will happen if they go to sleep in the dark, go near an insect, or forget to wash their hands.

Were you ever afraid of the dark?

Are you afraid of anything now?

There are two ways to get rid of the fears that you make up in your mind.

*You can grow out of the fear—or you can attack your fear—by doing the thing you are afraid of, and finding out that **nothing will happen!***

If you have a fear, you may draw a picture of yourself attacking your fear.

There are three parts to a fear:

> ***The Behavior**—What are you afraid to do?*
>
> ***The Thought**—Why are you afraid?*
>
> ***The Feeling**—What does it feel like to be afraid?*

When you change your behavior by attacking your fear, at first you will still have scary thoughts and uncomfortable feelings, but eventually the thoughts and feelings will also change.

The neat thing about having a fear is how much stronger you will become when you conquer your fear.

Draw a picture of yourself after the fear is gone.

Some children are afraid of what might happen when they are at home. They are afraid that they will be yelled at or that someone might hit them.

If you are afraid to be at home, you need to tell someone.

Sometimes children are afraid to tell someone for fear of being hurt because they told someone the secret that there was violence in the family.

If you are one of these children, don't be afraid to tell. There are people who will keep you and members of your family safe.

*What you need to know is that once you tell someone, the power of the secret is broken. Once the secret is out, **the abuse will stop.** So remember, **tell someone!***

A Workbook about Children Who are Special in Different Ways

From Now On
Summary—Where do we go from here?

From Now On

Books are written for many reasons.

Can you think of some of the reasons the author wrote this workbook?

What do you think he wanted you to remember?

How did he want your thinking to change?

Please don't turn the page until you have written all of your answers.

_____

_____

_____

_____

_____

_____

_____

*One reason he wrote the workbook was to make sure you knew about the word **empathy** and begin to use it when you deal with other people.*

*Another reason was to let you know that, if you are having problems such as the ones in this book, **you are not alone!***

*The last reason the author wrote this workbook was to get you to **stop and look at things differently.***

One way to look at things differently is to start to use empathy when dealing with others.

*Another way is to remember statements like: "**There is a light at the end of the tunnel or you can look at your cup as being half full rather than half empty.**"*

*These statements are called **metaphors** because they allow you to make a picture in your mind so that it becomes easier to remember an idea.*

*Another metaphor is: "**You need to walk in someone's shoes before you can really understand that person.**"*

What do you think that means?

*The most important metaphor is the act of **turning problems into gifts** so you can be wiser and stronger as a result of the problem.*

*The last metaphor the author would like you to remember is about opportunities: **"For every door that closes, another will open."***

What do you think that means?

After reading this workbook, you may know more things about a problem you are having. You may also have learned about the many different problems other children are having. The one thing you all have in common is that you all know how hard it is to be different in some way. What you may not have known is that having a handicap, a disability, or a rough time at home has made you stronger and better able to handle other problems in your life.

It may have been difficult to read some of the chapters in this book, but you did it! Congratulate yourself and your classmates for a job well done!